Concern for Animals

From a Catholic Perspective

by
Deborah M. Jones

*All booklets are published thanks to the
generous support of the members of the
Catholic Truth Society*

CATHOLIC TRUTH SOCIETY
PUBLISHERS TO THE HOLY SEE

Contents

Animals in our lives

Just what is it between so many of the saints and *animals*? There is St Mildred with her deer, St Hugh with his swan, St Roche with his dog, St Gerasimus with his lion - and many, many more. It would almost seem to be a condition of sanctity to have a special affinity with God's other creatures. And yet some Christians exclude animals from their religious concerns on the grounds that 'dumb beasts' are somehow unworthy of consideration or play no part in their lives. Meanwhile among the majority of Western households, at least one pet is considered to be a member of the family. Most people too regularly consume parts of animals, and wear animal skins on their feet. Most medicines they take and the household chemicals they use have been tested on animals. In any case, the moment anyone steps out of doors they enter the world of birds, insects, and all the species of wildlife. So animals really do play a significant part in our everyday lives, and the way we consider and treat them is a legitimate area for theological reflection.

Animals in history

From the earliest times mankind's fear of the dangerous wildness of animals was manifested in a need either to master them or to honour and appease them. Many ancient religions, for example the Egyptian, had animals as cult objects. To create one of the boundaries between these religions and their own, it was necessary for Israel (and early Christianity) to steer clear of all images and representations, including those of animals - to ensure that the mistake of the golden calf would not be repeated. Certain animals also came to be associated with diabolical imagery - such as cats, considered to be witches' 'familiars'.

'Give a dog a bad name, and hang it' is a truism born of experience: even today violent and unruly people are labelled 'animals', and people insult and dehumanise other folk by calling them the names of particularly despised animals. We associate some animals with aspects of ourselves that we most fear or want to control, (our animal instincts) and can boost our sense of superiority by expressing contempt for attitudes we consider to be sentimental.

Christian appreciation of animals

Within Israel's religion, as within Christianity, however, there has also been a tradition that has appreciated God's gift to us of the animal kingdom (the extent and beauty of which is made known to us more than ever before, through television). In this tradition, the virtues of gentleness and compassion are exercised towards all of

God's creatures, and the value of life itself as God's greatest gift to all living beings, both people and animal, is respected and cherished. Indeed to be truly pro-life, *all* life must be included or the concept of life itself is diminished and truncated. Catholic teaching has long enjoined consideration and positive kindness towards animals, supported by popes and cardinals, and exemplified by very many saints.

In a children's catechism published in London by the Catholic Truth Society in 1901, Bishop James Bellord, puts this question: 'Is cruelty to animals a sin?' The answer he gives is: 'Yes, a very cowardly and disgraceful sin'.

No-one but the most depraved person would disagree with that. But just what constitutes cruelty, and how and why it is sinful? Similar questions arise over certain paragraphs (namely numbers 2415-2418) in the more recent *Catechism of the Catholic Church* (1994); for example when it says that the infliction of unnecessary, or needless, suffering on animals is wrong. Just what suffering is 'unnecessary'? And what is implied by the terms it uses of 'stewardship', and 'dominion'? This little book attempts to shed some light on these and other questions.

The Bible and creation

In the first Genesis creation account, animals and people are created as 'living souls' to fill the earth, the air and the water, and to multiply. 'And God saw that [this creation] was good.' As a psalm relates, 'The Lord's tenderness embraces all his creatures' (*Ps* 145:9). They - including our human parents - are provided with a herbivorous diet and all live in harmony together. It is only with the onset of human sin that suffering, death and decay are introduced into nature. Israel's prophets look forward to the restoration of this original state, this peaceable Eden (see, *inter alia*, *Is* 11:5-9). This is ultimately to be achieved by the Son of God taking on human flesh, and giving his own life for the life of fallen creation. By becoming members of his risen body we are given a new way of living in, and relating to, the world, with the promise of a future when the whole of creation will one day be renewed - a future for which it is eagerly waiting (*Rm* 8:19-23). It is described in the Book of Revelation as the coming Kingdom of God, in which all created matter will glorify God in God's very presence. Around the heavenly throne are 'all the living things (Greek, *pan ktisima* = every creature) in creation - everything that lives in the air, and on the ground, and under the ground, and in the sea, crying, "To the One who is sitting on the throne and to the Lamb, be all praise, honour, glory and power, for ever and ever" (*Rv* 5:13).

Praising and glorifying God

This is the sweep of the Christian story - one that involves and concerns all living creatures, created for the glory and praise of God. Animals are not just part of the backdrop, the scenery before which the real story of human salvation takes place. The division between human and animal has been reconciled in Jesus Christ, who, while being truly divine yet was one in flesh with *all* that is fleshly. Pope John Paul II, in his 1980 encyclical *Dominum et Vivificantem* (n.50) was keen to emphasise this often overlooked theological point:

> The Incarnation of God the Son signifies the taking up into unity with God not only of human nature, but in this human nature, in a sense, of everything that is 'flesh': the whole of humanity, *the entire visible and material world*. The Incarnation, then, also has a cosmic significance, a cosmic dimension. The 'first-born of all creation', becoming incarnate in the individual humanity of Christ, unites himself in some way with the entire reality of man, which is also 'flesh' - and in this reality with *all 'flesh', with the whole of creation*.

As the 1994 *Catechism of the Catholic Church* puts it (n.2416) 'By their mere existence [animals] bless him and give him glory.' The fact that animals are innocent of sin, incapable of moral choices, means not that they are to be discarded as somehow worthless, but on the contrary, given divine value for just being what they are - as they naturally fulfil their purpose of praising God. (See *Ps* 147:7-10; 96:11-12; and particularly *Ps* 150, where

'everything that has breath' joins in noisy worship.)
Psalm 104 relates another creation account, telling in
dynamic fashion the concern that God the creator takes in
everything he has created.

God gives animals value

In other words, Scripture shows that animals have value
that is more than that placed on them by people. They are
valuable to God; they have value in and of themselves.
They are not ours, our property, our 'things' to do to as
we like. 'To The Lord belongs the earth and all it holds,
The world and all who live in it' (*Ps* 23:1); and,

Since all the forest animals are already mine,

And the cattle on my mountains in their thousands;

I know all the birds of the air,

nothing moves in the field that does not belong to me
(*Ps* 50:10-11)

In the Book of Job, chapters 38-42, God demands to
know of Job where he was when God set creation into
being, formed the animals and gave them their freedom.
Even the creation story in the first chapter of Genesis
does not culminate in the production of human beings -
brought into being on the same day as the other
mammals - but on the Sabbath of God, the point to
which all creation is oriented. In the New Testament too,
we find Jesus suggesting that his listeners 'Look at the

birds in the sky... your heavenly Father feeds them' (*Mt* 6:26). Even the death of a humble sparrow, almost without value to people (who can buy two for a penny), is noted by God (*Mt* 10:29). They have value for God. The *Catechism* notes (n.2416) that 'Animals are God's creatures. He surrounds them with his providential care.' The consequence of this is that we humans 'owe them kindness'.

Animals, God's own instruments

Animals can be God's own instruments, as when God spoke through Balaam's donkey (*Nb* 22:28-33). And animals are even used in Scripture as similes and metaphors of God's own self. In Hosea 13:7-8, God likens himself to a lion, a leopard, and a bear, and in Deuteronomy 32:11, to a protective eagle. In the New Testament too, the Third Person of the Trinity is likened to a gentle dove (*Mt* 3:16, *Jn* 1:32). Jesus likens himself to a mother hen wanting to gather her chicks (*Lk* 13:34).

Jesus himself was born in an animal stable, and early in his ministry spent forty days and nights in the company of wild beasts in the wilderness - a fact we will return to later. It was *everything* in creation for which Christ made peace, was reconciled by his death on the cross: all are brought together under Christ, as head, 'Everything in the heavens and everything on earth (*Col* 1:20 and *Ep* 1:10).

So God creates the animals, sustains them, relates with them, and saves them. After the terrible flood had destroyed the whole wicked generation of Noah's contemporaries, 'God had Noah in mind, and all the wild beats and all the cattle that were with him in the ark' (*Gn* 8:1). God's just anger too against the wickedness of Nineveh was deflected after the people and 'beasts, herds and flocks', together fasted in repentance; and God felt sorry for all the many ignorant people of Nineveh 'to say nothing of all the animals' (*Jon* 3:7, 4:11). Indeed, God made covenants directly with the animal creation.

Covenants with animals

Genesis 1:22 God blesses the creatures of the water and of the air, and bids them to reproduce. A few verses later, God blesses all the animals and human beings, and sets the human beings up as 'masters' of the creatures, giving them all vegetation to eat. The only acceptable model of 'master' known to the first people would be that of God himself. That is the meaning of the word 'dominion' - to be lords as God is Lord. So people are to be as loving and gracious to the creatures in their power as God is to them. They are made in God's image for that purpose - to be God's viceroys.

Genesis 9:9 After the flood, God establishes his covenant with Noah, his descendants, 'also with every living creature to be found with you, birds, cattle and every wild beast with you, everything that came out of the ark, everything that lives on the earth.' But with sin now an inbuilt part of the human condition, relationships between people, and between people and animals, will never again be as they were in Eden - until the Kingdom comes.

Hosea 4:20 The prophet Hosea describes the coming time when Israel shall return to God and God will renew his covenant with her, 'and with the wild animals, with the birds of heaven and the creeping things of the earth'. Note that these are not the animals that human beings tend to think of as important, such as pets, or food animals, but wild, flying and creeping things! It is not we who determine value, but God.

Animal sacrifice and Jesus,
the Sacrificial Lamb

It is often asked why, if animals were important to God,
they were sacrificed. Sacrificing animals to the gods was
a custom of most early societies, including those of the
Middle East. In the pastoral cultures, the killing of any
living creature was such an enormity that, before any was
killed, it was first offered back to its creator-god in
sacrifice. Only then could its flesh be eaten. As religions
developed, so did their motives and rituals for sacrifice -
usually to appease a vengeful god, or to become bonded
as a tribe or people with their god. Human beings too
were sacrificed in some cultures, with even the Israelites
succumbing to this Canaanite practice during their
wilderness wanderings (see *Ps* 106:36-39). However,
specific to the Israelites was the ban on consuming an
animal's blood out of respect for the life given to it by the
Creator. (We still call it 'life-blood'.) It was considered
'unclean' and incompatible with holiness to shed or
consume blood. Predatory animals ingest the blood of
others, so all such animals and birds were designated
non-kosher, or 'unclean', and forbidden to be eaten to this
day in Jewish culture.

The original sacrifices were local, taking place on temporary altars. However, animal sacrifices in Israel became highly organised, with holocausts (total burning of the carcass as the ultimate gift to God), and communion (meal) sacrifices (with the sharing of the meat bringing the people, the priests and God together into community). Eventually all religious ritual was centralised in one place, the Temple in Jerusalem. The courtyard outside the Holy of Holies became something of a mass slaughter-house, especially at Passover, with the priests performing the butchery and pouring the blood over the altar.

Jesus - the Sacrificial Lamb

When Jesus, the Paschal Lamb, died as the ultimate sacrificial victim, all other bloody sacrifices became instantly redundant in Christianity. 'He has entered the sanctuary once and for all, taking with him not the blood of goats and bull-calves, but his own blood, having won an eternal redemption for us' (*Heb* 9:12). In Judaism all sacrifices came to an end with the destruction of the Temple in AD 70 - being replaced by the 'spiritual sacrifices' of prayer and good works.

Other Old Testament attitudes to animals

Although animal sacrifice has been central to Temple worship, over time its deficiencies were increasingly recognised. The psalmist addressed God as wanting 'no sacrifice or oblation' and who 'asked for no holocaust or sacrifice for sin' (*Ps* 40:6). Animal sacrifice was insufficient in itself to gain atonement with God. Many of the prophets were insistent that God did not demand the sacrifice of animals, see Jeremiah 7:22, ff; Amos 5:21 ff, Isaiah 1:11 ff. What pleased God was the disposition of the human heart. Virtue is what matters, and 'The virtuous man looks after the life of his beasts, but the wicked man's heart is ruthless' (*Pr* 12:10). The commandments in Exodus include provision for Sabbath rest not only for people for also for their animals (*Ex* 20:10); and in Deuteronomy 25:4 threshers are instructed not to muzzle the oxen when they tread the corn, to allow them to graze as they work.

Such a respectful attitude towards animals continued into the Jewish tradition, given expression in *The Code of Jewish Law*, which states, 'It is forbidden, according to the law of the Torah, to inflict pain upon any living creature. On the contrary, it is our duty to relieve pain of any creature, even if it is ownerless or belongs to a non-Jew.' However strictly the rabbis interpret laws concerning the Sabbath, the obligation to relieve an animal from pain or danger supersedes them all, and all hunting is forbidden to Jews on the grounds of cruelty.

The world of the Roman Empire

When the early Christian Church moved away from its Jewish roots and spread throughout the Roman Empires of East and West, the Good News had to be expressed in terms that a wider community of people could comprehend. To do this, the thinking of the classical world had to become part of the Christian experience. Unfortunately for animals, the Greek and Roman philosophers drove a strong division between human beings and other creatures that continues largely to this day, and Christians were not immune from imbibing some of their attitudes. Known as 'anthropocentricism', or human-centredness, it is frequently and readily adopted even by kindly people who would otherwise consider the needs and welfare of others. It is somehow so imbedded in our culture that only a *metanoia*, complete change of heart and view, can dislodge it from its dominance.

Some key philosophers and movements

Socrates (469-399 BC) gave first expression to the concept of everything being created *solely* for the benefit of human beings. Even animals, he held, receive their life and food purely for the sake of human beings. This idea, which justifies the abuse of animals, was so readily taken up that it became considered self-evidently true. It remains the dominant view throughout much of the world.

Plato (428-348 BC) taught that all living creatures possess souls, animating (life-giving) principles, which even survive after death, but their reasoning faculties, like that of human slaves(!), were limited. To him rationality, the power of reasoning, was supreme. He opened up a controversy among classical philosophers as to which aspects of reasoning, among them memory, understanding, intuition, belief, expertise and technical knowledge, were unique to humans and which were shared with animals - a question that has not been settled even today, although ethologists struggle with it.

Aristotle (384-322 BC), Plato's famous pupil, granted animals - and even plants - the possession of souls (which give them life), and have consciousness, but held that their lack of rationality causes them to be denied the right to any kind of justice.

The Stoics (3rd century BC - AD 6th century) accepted Aristotle's denial of any justice to animals, teaching that animals are designed only for human benefit, and concluding that anything can be done to them with impunity. For one particular Stoic, **Chrysippus** (280-207 BC), everything was made for the sake of something else: plants for animals, and animals for people. People are here simply to observe and imitate the universe. A pig, to him, was given a living soul only to keep its meat from going off! It is but a step from that view to the mass industrial-scale 'hog farms' found, particularly in North Carolina and described in all their horrific detail in Matthew Scully's book *Dominion* (see Further Reading).

Saints and Animals

While the Church itself has not been immune from anthropocentrism, there have also been traditions going back to the earliest days which are more in tune with the biblical respect for God's creatures: the *anthropos* (human being) element being replaced with a more *theos* (God) - centred view of creation.

The Desert Fathers and the Celtic Saints

The ascetical movement of the early monastic Desert Fathers and Celtic saints resonates with one very powerful, yet tiny detail in the Gospel of Mark (1:12-13), mentioned above. This refers to Jesus being 'with the wild animals' in the wilderness. A Syriac homily by the fourth-century **St Ephrem** refers to Jesus being *at peace* with the wild animals 'which knelt and worshipped him'. Jesus is being supported not just by angels *but also* by wild animals. Just as Adam lived in harmony with all creatures, so here we have Jesus as the new Adam. Righteousness brings with it a peaceable existence with wild animals, just as Job was told that he 'shall not fear the wild animals of the earth… [They] shall be at peace with you' (*Jb* 5:22-23). In fact the whole messianic age, the coming Kingdom of God, would herald peace between animals and humans, as described in Isaiah 11:5-9.

In the many legends that sprang up in the early centuries of the Church, we see that really holy people anticipate and exemplify this messianic age in their own lives by their living peaceably with the wild animals of the desert. Two examples: **St Gerasimus**, a Palestinian monk of the fifth century treated a lion's paw in which a thorn had become embedded. The grateful lion then becomes the monk's assistant, responsible for and protecting the monastery's donkey. (Later Italian scribes confused the name 'Gerasimus' with 'Geronimo' - in English, **Jerome** - and the lion legend becomes associated with the biblical scholar **St Jerome** whose image in paintings from the 14th century onwards is always accompanied by a 'pet lion'.) **St Macarius** is a hermit living in a cave and is summoned by a hyena to attend to the blindness of her pups. By prayer and, in one account, spitting in the eyes (an obvious reference to Jesus' action in Mark 8:23 and John 9:6-7), the saint restores their sight. There are many such stories of the holiness of hermits and monks enabling wild animals to live in Eden-like harmony with them. Legends even sprang up of the lions in the arena being reluctant to kill the Christian martyrs thrown to them, as they respected, and even worshipped them, for their holiness. Typical is one where a lioness refused to devour the Cilician martyr,

St Aphrodisius - and then went on to stand on her hind legs and preach to the people, converting many!

A 7th century saint, **Isaac of Nineveh**, explained what happens when 'the humble man' approaches wild animals. They then behave like pet dogs.

> They scent as coming from him the same fragrance that came from Adam before the transgression, the time when they were gathered together before him and he gave them names in paradise. This scent was taken away from us, but Christ has renewed it and given it back to us at his coming.

The charitable heart

This saint also described the nature of the 'charitable heart' which every Christian aspires to develop. Its objects for love are entirely inclusive:

> What is a charitable heart? It is a heart which is burning with charity for the whole of creation, for men, for the birds, for the beasts, for the demons - for all creatures. He who has such a heart cannot see or call to mind a creature without his eyes becoming filled with tears by reason of the immense compassion which seizes his heart; a heart which is softened and can no longer bear to see or learn from others of any suffering, even the smallest pain, being inflicted upon a creature. That is why such a man never ceases to

pray also for the animals, for the enemies of truth, and for those who do him evil, that they may be preserved and purified. He will pray even for the reptiles, moved by the infinite pity which reigns in the hearts of those who are becoming united to God.

The Celtic saints, following the ascetical rigour of the Eastern hermits and monastics also demonstrated close bonds with wild animals, **St Kevin**, on whose outstretched hands a blackbird makes a nest, lays an egg, and hatches it - while the saint does not move a muscle! Another is **St Cuthbert** who prays all night standing in the North Sea. When he moves to the beach, two sea-otters come ashore, lick his feet, and dry and warm them with their fur and breath.

St Irenaeus and St Benedict

This restoration of the right order of creation, anticipated by certain remarkable saints, is given theological underpinning by **St Irenaeus** (c.130-200). He taught that the reward for a holy life is a bodily resurrection, linked with the final restoration of the whole creation to a new Eden in its 'primeval condition'. At the time of Irenaeus there were many influential movements that over-emphasised the spiritual dimension, so that his concentration on the material, the body and the earthly creation was necessary to restore balance. It is the physical reality that is to be transformed, or 'set free' (*Rm* 8:20-21).

The movement of withdrawal and solitude of the Desert Fathers in the East (Egypt, Syria, etc) gave place in the West to more settled community living, led by **St Benedict of Nursia** (c.480-550), known as the Founder of Western Monasticism. His 1896 biographer, Abbot Tosti, writes of how Benedict made friends with the wildlife near his monastery:

> Men like St Benedict, always intent on the love of the Creator, could not withhold their love from the things He had created. Hence they felt themselves bound by the bonds of fraternal love with everything in God's universe. On the other hand, the irrational animals, by divine ordination, often gave their services to these holy men, who, in the desert, far from human society, committed their lives into the hands of God alone.

St Francis and St Philip Neri

The 1994 Catechism picks out two saints, from the very many available, to exemplify the right relationship with animals: 'We should recall the gentleness with which saints like St Francis of Assisi or St Philip Neri treated animals' (n.2416). How, apart from gently, did these two men treat them?

St Francis of Assisi (1181-1226) views the whole of creation as sacramental, a sign of the holy. To him, God is revealed and encountered in the mountains, the hills, the trees, the animals, as well as in humans. All creatures are to be respected and cherished as related family members, as kin, as we all share the same divine Creator-Father. He calls each creature Brother and Sister, and treats them fondly, preaching to the birds, and saving the life of a wolf, a rabbit, a fish, and many others, which were drawn to him as the wild animals were to the Desert Fathers. In Francis' view of the world, there is no hierarchy involved; animals and humans are equal in it. In the first enactment of the nativity story in a live crib-scene with human actors in a stable, Francis introduced an ox and an ass - missing from the Gospel accounts, but referred to in Isaiah 1:3 as knowing their owner and 'their master's crib', whereas God's people did not know or understand. An ox and an ass have featured ever since in nativity scenes. St Francis is held up as the ultimate 'friend of animals' and is universally popular, even among people with no other religious interest.

The interest in animals of **St Philip Neri** (1515-1595) the founder of the Oratory movement, are far less well known. He was a vegetarian, declaring once, on passing a butcher's shop, 'If everyone were like me, they wouldn't kill animals'. He also bought birds in cages, in order to set them free, and gave away donated game birds so they could be kept alive. He shooed flies out of the window instead of swatting them, and released captured mice into places of safety for them. His cat at San Girolamo was known to all Rome. Such concern for animals was remarkable in the 16th century.

St Matin de Porres, St Ciaran and St Basil the Great

St Martin de Porres (1579-1639), a Dominican Tertiary, who lived in the great convent of Lima, Peru, used to feed rats and mice at the end of the monastery garden, but forbade them to enter the building. He made a sanctuary-hospital for lost dogs and cats and all sorts of suffering animals. When his patients became too many, he lodged them in his sister's house and attended them daily. Like so many people who care for animals, he did not neglect needy human beings, and founded hospitals for the poor. Another shining example of this is **St Ciaran (Kieran) of Clonmacnoise** (c.512-c.545), of whom it was said he was 'like a burning lamp of charity, so rare that not only did the fervour and devotion of his pitiful heart go out to the relieving of the hunger of men, but he showed himself tireless in caring for dumb beasts in their necessity'. Finally, **St Basil the Great** (c.330-379), Metropolitan of Caesarea, saw the natural world as revealing the beauty and power of God. His prayer, from the Russian liturgy, is worth reporting in full as the first recorded expression of shame for human cruelty to animals:

> The Earth is the Lord's and the fulness thereof. O God, enlarge within us the sense of fellowship with all

living things, our brothers the animals to whom thou hast given the earth as their home in common with us. We remember with shame that in the past we have exercised the high dominion of man with ruthless cruelty, so that the voice of the earth. which should have gone up to thee in song, has been a groan of travail. May we realise that they live, not for us alone, but for themselves and for thee, and that they have the sweetness of life.

Another of his liturgical prayers speaks of God having saved both man and beast, 'We pray thee, O Lord, for the humble beasts... and for the wild animals, whom thou hast made, strong and beautiful; we supplicate for them thy great tenderness of heart, for thou hast promised to save both man and beast...'

Popes and Animals

In 1567, in the papal bull, *De Salute Gregis*, **Pope (later, Saint) Pius V**, prohibited watching or taking part in bull-fighting, 'as being contrary to Christian duty and charity'. A later pope was persuaded by Philip II of Spain to lift the excommunication penalties, although monks and friars were still subject to them. However, Pope Benedict XV in 1920 confirmed Pius V's bull to be 'the mind of the Church', as it is:

> Altogether in the spirit of our Holy Books, which call upon even wild animals to bless the good God, and wholly accords with the gentle law of Him Who has deigned to call Himself the Lamb of God... And if, in spite of the spirit of humanity which the New Law encourages, human savagery falls away again in the promotion of bull-fights, there is no doubt that the Church continues, as she has done in the past, loudly to condemn these shameful and bloody spectacles.

When **Pope Leo XIII** (r.1878-1903) became patron of the French Society for the Prevention of Cruelty to Animals, Cardinal Donnet announced that 'The Church, by the voice of her Sovereign Pontiffs, has placed herself at the head of the movement. It is for her to take the lead whenever she can make herself heard.' Leo's successor, **Pope Pius X** (r.1903-1914), sent the French SPCA an autographed blessing 'for all who protect from abuse and cruelty the dumb servants given to us by God', and wished 'prosperity and success to all workers in this field.' He declared himself pleased to support 'so noble an undertaking, which has the lofty object of caring for the lives and treatment of animals and which at the same time endeavours to eradicate from the hearts of men barbarous tendencies'.

During the horrors of the First World War, **Pope Benedict XV** wrote to the head of the Italian Society for the Prevention of Cruelty to Animals:

> His Holiness rejoices to know that the object of your Society is in perfect accord with the doctrine which the Church has always taught and the Saints have always followed, leaving us innumerable beautiful examples of compassion and tenderness.

> The fact that the Nations have not always followed the precepts of the Church and the example of the Saints moves the Sovereign Pontiff all the more to favour all that tends… to foster respect for these other creatures of God, which Providence forbids us to exploit without concern and enjoins us to show wisdom in our use of them…

Therefore the August Pontiff trusts that you will find faithful and efficient fellow-workers in the priests of God, since it is their duty to conform to the teaching of the Church and the example of the Saints.

It is for them nobly to train souls in sentiments of enlightened gentleness and fostering care and guidance, so that they may offer to the animals refuge from every suspicion of roughness, cruelty or barbarism, and lead men to understand from the beauty of creation something of the infinite perfection of the Creator.

Papal pronouncements in modern times

Following the example set by **Pope Paul II** (r.1464-71) in rescuing and releasing animals and birds intended for the table, **Pius XII** (r.1939-1958), rescued a wounded bullfinch in the Vatican grounds and nursed it back to health. While he refused to meet Spanish bull-fighters, he did give an audience in November 1950 to the Duchess of Hamilton, who represented two hundred British animal welfare charities. He told her that:

The animal world, as all creation, is a manifestation of God's power, His wisdom and His goodness, and as such deserves our respect and our consideration. Any reckless desire to kill animals, all unnecessary harshness and callous cruelty towards them are to be condemned... The Catholic Church strives to influence individuals and pubic opinion to ensure the acceptance of these principles and their protection in daily life.

While opening 1950 Holy Year, the Pope declared that 'cruelty to animals is sinful', and appealed to the people of Rome to mark St Francis' Day by providing their animals with a feast. **John XXIII** (r.1958-1963), warned members of a conference of hydatidologists (specialists in tapeworm diseases, transmitted from sheep to dogs to people), that as 'sheep and dogs also are God's creatures' they are not to be ill-treated in the course of their researches. In 1967, **Paul VI** (r.1963-1978) received a delegation from the UK-based Catholic Study Circle for Animal Welfare (now known as Catholic Concern for Animals) and told them that their 'lofty goals … reflect in a very beautiful way the gentle love which is an important fruit of Christian charity' and that what they seek to accomplish 'is in conformity with the ends which God had in creating this world …'. In the book *Love and Responsibility*, written before he became **Pope John Paul II**, Karol Wojtyla wrote: 'In his treatment of animals in particular, since they are beings endowed with feeling and sensitive to pain, man is required to ensure that the use of these creatures is never attended by suffering or physical torture'. (Trans. by HT Willetts, Fount paperback, 1982. p. 25).

Animal Rights

Do animals have rights? Obviously they do not in the sense of being entitled to vote or to be expected to discharge duties - any more than are infant children. But St Thomas Aquinas affirmed that they do indeed have natural rights, defended by justice. In God's world of nature, all creatures obey eternal law, defined as God's 'wisdom directing all actions and movements' (*Summa Theol*.2.1.93.1). This eternal law, which science can discover, this *jus* in Latin, is the object of justice, or doing what is right. The first principle of it is to do good and avoid evil. Justice defends natural rights, which go before mere man-made laws. We can tell what the natural laws are by close observation - and ethology (the science of animal behaviour) is discovering more all the time. Every animal achieves its God-given purpose, its *telos*, through the behaviour that is natural to it. This is what the Catechism means in n. 2416 where it says that by animals' 'mere existence, they bless God and give him glory'. So our treatment of each animal should enable it to achieve its purpose and not prevent it from fulfilling it. The Catholic theologian, Richard Wade, condemns any violation of the natural inclinations of animals:

for example, [by] the infliction of pain and abuse,
deprivation of water, food, space to run free, and so
forth, is against the interests they require to have their
natures fulfilled ... Failure to respect the *prima facie*
interests of animals based upon their nature is to deny
them natural justice.

(From *Towards a Christian Ethic of Animals*, Pacifica
13.2 (June 2000), pp.202-212.)

The Catechism on animals

The Catechism (n.2415) upholds this view by stating that,
'Man's dominion over inanimate and other living beings
granted by the Creator is not absolute... it requires a
religious respect for the integrity of creation'. This means
that we cannot do just as we please with created beings.
To achieve a 'religious respect' implies more than simply
following the basic requirements of care for living
creatures. It is to acknowledge that, as St Francis
testified, we all have a common Father-Creator. It is
God's rights that are trampled when his beloved creation
is misused and abused. As Cardinal John C. Heenan of
Westminster wrote in replying to the proposition that
animals have no rights:

they have very positive rights because they are God's
creatures. If we have to speak with absolute accuracy

we must say that God has the right to have all his
creatures treated with proper respect.

Nobody should therefore careless repeat the old saying
that animals have no rights. This could easily lead to
wanton cruelty ... the rights of God can be
transgressed through ignorance as well as malice.
(Foreword to *God's Animals*, by Dom Ambrose Agius
OSB, Catholic Study Circle for the Welfare of Animals
(June 1970), p.2.)

The Christian duty of kindness

The Cardinal showed how the Christian duty of kindness
is developed from these rights. He mentioned the nature
of cruelty - that much of it is practised as 'a matter of
business', rather than deliberately (except by 'the
perverted') - and then stated:

It was once pointed out to me that the catechism [the
Penny Catechism of 1911] had no question about
cruelty to animals. This was true but in giving lessons
on Christian doctrine teachers now include the subject
of cruelty to animals. The best and most experienced
teachers do not, of course, talk of cruelty to animals.
They talk of kindness to animals. Christians have a
duty not only to refrain from doing harm but also to do
positive good.

A previous Cardinal Archbishop of Westminster, Francis Bourne (1861-1935), in a talk to children in Westminster Cathedral in April 1931, said 'There is even in kindness to animals a special merit in remembering that this kindness is obligatory upon us because God made the animals, and is, therefore, their Creator.'

However awesome and beautiful, nature is not an end in itself, but its *telos*, its purpose, goal, or destined end the *telos* of every created thing, is the worship of God. In St Thomas Aquinas' own words:

> Therefore, in the parts of the universe also every creature exists for its own proper act and perfection... whilst each and every creature exists for the sake of the universe. Furthermore, the entire universe, with all its parts, is ordained towards God as its end, inasmuch as it imitates, as it were, and shows forth the Divine goodness, to the glory of God... Thus it is plain that Divine goodness is the end of all corporeal beings. (*Summa Theol.* I.65.2)

What then is the appropriate treatment of animals?

As Christians we want to follow more closely the example set by Our Lord and his saints - to live gently, compassionately and mercifully. By exercising the virtues of faith, hope and charity, temperance, prudence, justice, and fortitude, we can develop a character that, fortified by prayer and the sacraments, will make the right choices naturally and spontaneously. Most of us however need some help in determining what those right choices are, and certain principles may guide us.

The Catechism sets out two general principles. One is that, because 'animals are God's creatures... Thus men owe them kindness' (n.2416). The other is that 'It is contrary to human dignity to cause animals to suffer or die needlessly' (n.2418). Note the important word 'needlessly'. Real need or necessity is the only appropriate reason for causing suffering or death to animals. Much of what we do to animals is to satisfy some requirement that is much less than need, such as taste, convention, entertainment, convenience, and so on. Need implies that without which we cannot live, not just something that we enjoy.

Another principle we can bear in mind in this respect is the one expressed in Catechism n.1756: 'One may not do evil so that good may result from it'. We can also ask ourselves whether there is due proportion involved. For example, if we cause more harm than the benefits warrant, that would constitute an unacceptable action. St Thomas Aquinas expressed this as follows:

And yet, though proceeding from a good intention, an act may be rendered unlawful, if it be out of proportion to the end... Wherefore, if a man, in self-defence, uses more than necessary violence, it will be unlawful: whereas if he repel force with moderation it will be lawful (*Summa Theol.*, P.II-II, Q.64. Art.7).

The choice we make therefore must be the option 'which represents the least destruction of good possible under the circumstances'. How that is worked out in practice is suggested here.

Dogs, cats and other pet animals

Dogs and cats have long been domesticated - literally, trained to live with us in our 'domus'. Their human carers are entirely responsible for their welfare. Dog owners are morally obliged to see that, as natural pack animals related to wolves, dogs are not left alone, nor expected to behave as 'little people'. Owners of cats need to protect the local wildlife, and not let their cats stay outdoors in twilight or darkness. The Catechism (n.2418) warns against spending money on them that should 'as a priority go to the relief of human misery'. Spending disproportionate amounts of money on pet 'clothing'; jewelled collars, or fancy foods is an abuse of resources - as, of course, is any spending on frivolous luxury. What is more, is that the dignity of the pet as an animal is compromised. Where once it was taught that it is not possible for humans to share fellowship with 'irrational' animals, the Catechism goes on to declare that one can indeed love animals, although not in the way that one loves another person. Indeed, research suggests that being responsible for, and loving pets in childhood, helps a person to develop the empathy needed as an adult to relate in a healthy, responsible and sensitive way to other people. To avoid pet animals being killed or abandoned as strays, it is better to adopt them from rescue centres than to buy them from breeders, and to ensure that animals which would live in packs or herds would not be kept in solitary conditions, nor birds in cages, nor fish in small bowls.

Some Catholics sadly misapply the Church's teaching on birth control to animals, allowing their unneutered dogs and cats to produce innumerable offspring. Of course the Church's teaching on sexuality does not apply to animals, since animals engage in the sexual act purely driven by instinct as opposed to humans whose actions also fall within the moral sphere. Euthanasia is another case. An animal can be legitimately and humanely administered with painkillers to alleviate its sufferings, even where death is a foreseen and tolerated inevitability. In fact this is the same situation as it is with people (see *CCC* n. 2279). But this is quite different from 'putting down' a healthy animal, which would indeed be cruel and wrong.

What we eat

The Church has not pronounced on the subject of killing animals for food - either for or against. In 1992, when still a cardinal, Pope Benedict XVI was asked in an interview with a journalist, whether killing animals for food is permissible. His answer echoes a point often made by Christian promoters of vegetarianism that, at first, the only food provision for human beings was plant-life: 'Only after the flood, that is to say, after a new breach has been opened between God and man, are we told that man eats flesh...'. (Joseph Ratzinger, *God and the World, a conversation with Peter Seewald*, translated by Henry Taylor. San Francisco: Ignatius Press, 2002, p.79). So killing for food has not been forbidden although, he insists, a person 'should always maintain his respect for these creatures'.

Carnivores or herbivores?

The Catechism requirement not to cause the unnecessary suffering or death of animals (n.2418) could indicate that, as meat-eating is not necessary for a healthy diet for most people, vegetarianism is recommended. Indeed the Church has a long ascetical tradition of self-denial, whereby people, including several religious orders, renounce meat-eating in order to live a more simple life-style, in solidarity with the poorest people. For centuries the faithful abstained from meat-eating on Fridays, also some on Wednesdays, and during Lent and Advent, although often fish was substituted for the flesh of mammals and birds. Nowadays many organisations concerned with both global social justice and the environment urge the reduction or elimination of a meat-based diet in order to be able to feed growing human populations in a world of limited resources, and to cut down our 'carbon footprint'. It is estimated that livestock consume at least three times (some say seven times or more) the amount of food that they return in the form of meat, eggs and milk; and their sector accounts for up to one fifth of all greenhouse gas emissions.

Animals on farms

Despite the implications for human health, climate change, social justice etc, meat-eating is increasing world-wide. So the welfare and comfort of the animals used for food, both in their lives and in the manner of their deaths, must be a high priority. Dr Marie Hendrickx, of the Vatican's Congregation for Doctrine of the Faith, seriously challenged today's industrial treatment of animals:

> Does the right to use animals for food imply the right to raise chickens in tiny cages where they live in a

space smaller than a notebook? Or calves in compartments where they can never move about or see the light? Or to keep sows pinned by iron rings in a feeding position to allow a series of piglets to suck milk constantly and thus grow faster? ('For a More Just Relationship with Animals', *L'Osservatore Romano*, 24th January 2001).

Similarly, Pope Benedict XVI, in the 1992 interview, gives a powerful denunciation of certain farming practices, namely the method of producing foie gras, and intensive poultry conditions:

Certainly, a sort of industrial use of creatures, so that geese are fed in such a way as to produce as large a liver as possible, or hens live so packed together that they become just caricatures of birds, this degrading of living creatures to a commodity seems to me in fact to contradict the relationship of mutuality that comes across in the Bible. (*God and the World*, see above, p.79).

Standards of animal welfare

A minimum standard of welfare for farm animals would require the full implementation of the 'Five Freedoms', a code of the Farm Animal Welfare Council: freedom from hunger and thirst; from discomfort; from pain, injury and disease; from fear and distress, and the freedom to express normal behaviour, which includes providing sufficient space, proper facilities and the company of the animal's own kind. These conditions would prevent the 'farming' of basically wild animals for fur - and the day will come when trapping too will be considered as having no place in the modern world, where substitute furs both look and feel similar to the real thing.

In poor and developing countries, animals such as donkeys, camels, oxen and llamas are used for carrying loads and for pulling ploughs, carts and so on. Their owners benefit when animal welfare standards are raised, either by education or other support. Often however there has built up a culture of indifference to animal suffering, one which the Church needs to address as part of its mission to the poor.

Wild animals

We human beings increasingly destroy the balance of nature, for example, by eliminating many natural predators and habitats. So the responsibility for the welfare of certain wild species falls on us. When they are threatened by disease or over-population, we should, if we can, treat the sick animals and relocate excess numbers. Where we cannot, we have, regrettably, to resort to culling of the weakest and sickest, but only by expert and authorised marksmen. To destroy any of God's creatures for 'sport' or 'recreation' are activities no

Christian or humane person could consider; although hunting for food - where other sources of protein are genuinely not available - would come under the category of 'self-defence', one life taken so that another may survive. Since AD 830 the clergy have been forbidden to hunt. In the *Roman Penitential of Halitgar*, published in France, clergy of every rank were banned from hunting, with the penance tariff set for two years for deacons and three for priests.

Animal experimentation

The Catechism n.2417 states that 'Medical and scientific experimentation on animals is a morally acceptable practice if it remains within reasonable limits and contributes to caring for or saving human lives.' However, it does not specify what constitutes 'reasonable limits', and whatever conditions they are kept in, the animals' lives are intentionally shortened and frequently subjected to pain and suffering. Some would argue that the price is worth paying, even if the cost is all on one side and the benefit all on the other. Some major achievements in surgical, medical and pharmaceutical fields have resulted from the use of animals. However some advances have been held back or the resultant drugs or procedures proved actually dangerous, as animals' systems and reactions often differ widely from those of human beings.

While the Catechism accepts a modified form of the situation that exists, there have been Catholic voices, notably British ones, that have spoken out against the practice. Cardinal John Henry Newman, in his 1842 Good Friday sermon, preached movingly about cruelties exercised on animals, including the use of live animals in experiments, known as 'vivisection':

> At one time it is the wanton deed of barbarous and angry owners who ill treat their cattle or beasts of burden; and at another it is the cold blooded and calculating act of men of Science, who make experiments on animals, perhaps merely from a sort of curiosity.

He makes a daring comparison between the suffering of animals and that of Christ's suffering on the cross:

> Think then of your feelings at cruelty practiced upon brute animals, and you will gain one sort of feeling which the history of Christ's Cross and Passion ought to excite within you...let them remind you, as a picture, of Christ's sufferings. He who is higher then the angels, deigned to humble himself even to the state of the brute creation...

and concludes that:

> There is something so very dreadful, so satanic in tormenting those who have never harmed us, and who

cannot defend themselves, who are utterly in our power, who have weapons neither of offence nor defence, that none but very hardened persons can endure the thought of it.

Catholic intervention

In 1875, Cardinal Manning and others were so horrified at the practice that they formed the Victoria Street Society which, from 1897, has been known as the National Anti-Vivisection Society. As vice-president, he made frequent speeches against the 'detestable practice' which he considered 'immoral in itself', including the following:

> this I do protest, that there is not a religious instinct in nature, nor a religion of nature, nor is there a word in revelation, either in the Old Testament or the New Testament, nor is there to be found in the great theology which I do represent, nor in any Act of the Church of which I am a member; nor in the lives and utterances of any one of those great servants of that Church who stand as examples, nor is there an authoritative utterance anywhere to be found in favour of vivisection.

There are agencies and institutions which do not use animals and seek viable alternatives. Catholic academic and research institutions could join this trend and call for an immediate end of all unnecessarily repeated experiments. As the Church is rightly cautious about the growth of bioengineering, it would further safeguard the human person by upholding the integrity of creation in relation to the genetic engineering, modification or cloning of any animal. Changes to the genetic constitution of any creature, other than occur naturally or by natural processes, trespass against the divine law and intention for that creature.

Animals used for entertainment

Horse racing is a very popular pastime, and many people see no harm in 'a little flutter', especially at the Grand National. While they see horses being whipped and many suffering fatal falls, they may not be aware of the 'behind the scenes' cruelty involved. Horses and greyhounds in the racing industry are bred to unnatural standards and, if not selected or when they have finished their racing lives, are often discarded and abandoned, or worse. Even ponies and horses used for innocent recreation may be kept in conditions that are far from natural for social, herd animals. Circuses and similar entertainments, at worst, cruelly exploit animals and at best compromise their dignity. Many zoos have improved their welfare standards, providing space and conditions more closely replicating each species' natural environment, but many, even in Western Europe, are appalling. Today's visual media have eliminated the educational need for such places, and only outstanding conservation requirements can justify them.

A general approach to all animals: stewardship

To fulfil the Catechism's injunction to have respect for the integrity of creation (n.2415), what should be our general approach to the treatment of any animal? One significant term provided by the Catechism is that of 'stewardship'. In n.2402, (similarly in n.2415) we read that all creation has been put into the hands of the human race: 'In the beginning God entrusted the earth and its resources to the common stewardship of mankind to take care of them, master them by labour, and enjoy their fruits'. The stewardship approach is a care-taking one, a looking after something on behalf of someone else - biblically, an absent master or landlord. We know that God, the master of all, is not absent, but yet delegates to human beings the physical care of his creation - and to do it in the way that God Himself would. The way God treats animals is expressed in the Catechism, n.2416: 'He surrounds them with his providential care'. God is not absent from his world of creatures, they are not abandoned once they have been created. In paragraph n.301, God not only:

Gives them being and existence, but also, and at every moment, upholds and sustains them in being, enables them to act and brings them to their final end. Recognising this utter dependence with respect to the Creator is a source of wisdom and freedom, of joy and confidence.

It then quotes in length from Wisdom 11:24-26:

For you love all things that exist, and detest none of the things that you have made; for you would not have made anything if you had hated it. How would anything have endured, if you had not willed it? Or how would anything not called forth by you have been preserved? You spare all things, for they are yours, O Lord, you who love the living.

As stewards, we will be called to account for our treatment of God's creation, and God's beloved world of animals. An early Dominican writer (possibly St Thomas Aquinas himself), wrote this:

It is God's custom to care for all his creatures, both the greatest and the least. We should likewise care for creatures, whatsoever they are, in the sense that we use them in conformity with the divine purpose, in order that they may not bear witness against us on the day of judgement....

(Aquinas, *De cura Dei de creaturis*, in *De divinis moribus* from *Opusculum LXII, Omnia Opera*, Vol.28.)

Care and dominion

This idea of our being accountable was expressed three hundred years ago by the Catholic poet, Alexander Pope, writing:

> I cannot think it extravagant to imagine that mankind are no less, in proportion, accountable for the ill-use of their dominion over creatures of the lower rank of beings, than for the exercise of tyranny over their own species. (*Of Cruelty to Animals, A Hundred English Essays*, edited by R. Vallance (London: Thos. Nelson & Sons, 1950), p.159.)

In the Roman Missal 3rd edition (2011), there is a link between care and 'dominion': 'You formed man in your own image, and entrusted the whole world to his care, so that in serving you alone, the Creator, he might have dominion over all creatures'. It is remembered that 'dominion' in the Christian sense is one of service and sacrifice - following the example of Christ, the servant-king.

Why are we stewards or servant-kings of creation? The liturgy offers some explanations: in one of the optional prefaces for Sunday Eucharistic prayers (V) the purpose of the stewardship of creation is continuously to give praise for it. Addressing God: 'You made man the steward of creation, / to praise you day by day for the marvels of your wisdom and power / through Jesus Christ our Lord'; and in Eucharistic Prayer III, we are witnesses to the fact that 'all creation rightly gives you praise'. In the 3rd edition, the wording is: 'all you have created rightly gives you praise' and it goes on to say that 'You give life to all things and make them holy'. All things, all creatures, are 'made holy' by the gift of the divine life within them. So it follows that the more that creation is enabled to flourish, the more it is able to do what it is intended to do - to praise God. To repeat the phrase in the Catechism: 'By their mere existence [animals] bless him and give him glory' n.2416.

God's purpose for living creatures

So the purpose of each animal is just as it is for us - to give glory to God. Whilst we may, under strict conditions, use certain animals, they do not exist for us, but for themselves and for God. There is so much variety in nature 'because His goodness could not be adequately represented by any one creature alone, He produced many and diverse creatures, that what was wanting to one in the representation of the divine goodness could be supplied by another' (Aquinas, *Summa Theol.*I.47.1). As each creature reflects the likeness of God, so it also receives the love of God - as expressed in the preface to Eucharistic Prayer IV: 'Source of life and goodness, you have created all things, / to fill your creatures with every blessing' [3rd edition, 2011, 'you...the source of life, have made all that is, so that you might fill your creatures with blessings']. The way we are to treat all creatures is in terms of our obligation to our merciful, compassionate God. In the words of Cardinal Manning:

> We owe a seven-fold obligation to the Creator of those animals. Our obligation and moral duty is to Him who made them and if we wish to know the limit and the broad outline of our obligation, I say at once it is His nature and His perfections, and among these perfections one is, most profoundly, that of eternal mercy... (From *The Zoophilist*, London, 1st April 1887).

Basically, as the Russian writer Dostoevsky put into the mouth of Father Zossima, 'Love animals, love plants, love each thing. If you love each thing you will perceive the mystery of God in things', (F. Dostoevsky: *The Brothers Karamazov*, London: Vintage, 2004, p. 319).

Mankind's priesthood of creation

In Eucharistic Prayer IV in the 1970 Roman Missal, the worshipper praises God's glory *'in the name of every creature under heaven...'* [3rd edition: 'giving voice to every creature under heaven']. It seems therefore that the Christian has not only a responsibility to God by the compassionate treatment of animals, but also a priestly role in representing the whole living world by offering praise to God. At the Eucharist, we present this world, the fallen world, to God who then transforms it. This transformation of 'the whole creation' is described in Romans 8:19-25 as the freedom of all creatures from the cycle of sin and death into a glorious new life. It is expressed in the Intercessions in Eucharistic Prayer IV (3rd edition, 2011) as: 'There [in your kingdom], with the whole of creation, freed from the corruption of sin and death, may we glorify you..'. There is the answer to the much-asked question: 'Will my dog/cat/rabbit go to heaven?' While we cannot know for certain what takes place immediately after death, we do have the assurance that all creatures, and that includes the dogs and rabbits, will ultimately enter the glory that is God's kingdom. If we, in our limited way, can love them, how much more does their Creator-God? To counter the notion that 'animals do not have souls', Pope John Paul II declared in a public audience on 19th January, 1990 that 'also the animals possess a soul and men must love and feel solidarity with our smaller brethren'. He went on to state that all animals are the 'fruit of the creative action of the Holy Spirit and merit respect' and that they are 'as near to God as men are'. After quoting from Psalm 104, he concluded that 'all living creatures depend on the living spirit/breath of God that not only creates but also sustains and renews the face of the earth'. It is surely in the power of the Creator to grant salvation to all of his own creation. To think otherwise would be to belittle and confine infinite God.

Christ - head of Creation

Christ is the head of this creation; as the representative and perfect Man he is the 'world's High Priest' who, according to the poet George Herbert, 'doth present / The sacrifice for all' (From *Providence*). Through him, perfect Man and perfect God, earth and heaven come together. As the Solemn Blessing at Christmas Midnight Mass expresses it, 'When the Word became man, earth was joined to heaven'. Jesus Christ shares flesh with all that is fleshly - human and animal - and thus brings divinity to mere matter. How then can living elements of that matter, the whole diversity of animal creation, be dismissed as of

no importance, or of importance only to the extent that
we can make them serve our needs?

Liturgical hospitality

Farm animals have been blessed in Rome and other
places in the Mediterranean world for hundreds of
years, on the 17th January, the Feast of St Anthony of
Egypt, and now are joined by pets. The blessing of
animals in churches and cathedrals is becoming a
widespread tradition in the rest of the world, but
usually on or about the 4th October, the Feast of St
Francis of Assisi. In one Roman church, San Giovanni
dei Fiorentini, the late parish priest, Monsignor
Canciani, long welcomed animals and blessed them.
After the 1990 papal audience mentioned above, Mgr
Canciani was interviewed for an Italian magazine. He
said that:

> When the Pope stated that 'also the animals possess a
> soul and that men must love and feel solidarity with
> our smaller brethren', I felt greatly moved. At last my
> work for the world of animals had been rewarded. I
> have welcomed my parishioners into church for Mass
> accompanied by their dogs, cats and other faithful
> animal friends for a number of years because I have
> long recognised the justice in maintaining that all

God's creatures have the right to approach their Creator. And I now bless animals and their owners twice a year during a special Mass because all creatures have the right to feel loved by God and be near Him.' (*Gente*, also in *Man/Nature/Animals*, January 1990).

Forms of prayer for animals

But there are other ways that the Church could provide help to people, such as providing forms of prayer for those suffering the loss of a beloved pet, and for the disposal of its remains. For people who depend on the company of their animal friends, such a loss is real and heart-breaking. A prayer of blessing could be said also to welcome a new pet into a family. Prayers for farm animals would remind people of the fact that they are not unfeeling commodities, but living beings, lent by God.

There are various days in the calendar which are traditionally celebrated by people concerned with animals, such as Animal Welfare Sunday, nearest to the Feast of St Francis, and the Orthodox Church's 'Feast of Creation' on 1st September, initiated in 1989, which the Church could adopt to show solidarity with animals and those concerned for them.

Catechesis and theology

Attention can also be given to developing catechetical and teaching materials which build on the child's ready interest in animals. They can be helped to see animals as God's creatures put into their care. Seminary and tertiary education too, could accept the subject of animals as a serious subject for study in theology as well as in ethics. There is much research work to be done on the connection between violence to animals and to people; on ethics and bioethics relating to the use of animals; on the link between saints and animals, and on the development of animal theology.

Practical action

Most practically, Christian families, parishes, schools etc could lead the rest of society by their notably ethical use of animals for food, sport and recreation. For example all parish functions, as well as the catering being Fair Trade, could also be Cruelty Free. Perhaps also we could consider whether attendance at horse and dog races the wearing of (real) fur coats, the patronage of pet animal breeders, and so forth, are truly compatible with the Catechism's call that we should treat animals 'with kindness' and with the gentleness of the saints. Thus would attention be drawn to the triangular relationship - between people, God and animals - that is truncated whenever one of those elements is missing or misplaced.

Useful links

Catholic Concern for Animals, 15 Rosehip Way, Bishops Cleeve, Cheltenham GL52 8WP - *www.catholic-animals.org* (Reg.Charity 231022)

Further reading

The School of Compassion: a Roman Catholic Theology of Animals, by Deborah M Jones. Leominster: Gracewing, 2009.

Dominion: the Power of Man, the Suffering of Animals, and the Call to Mercy, by Matthew Scully. New York: St Martin's Press, 2002.

Ethics, Humans and other Animals: an Introduction with Readings, by Rosalind Hursthouse. The Open University. London: Routledge, 2000.

Any of the books by Andrew Linzey: for example -

Creatures of the Same God: Explorations in Animal Theology. Winchester University Press, 2007

Animal Gospel: Christian Faith as Though Animals Mattered, London: Hodder & Stoughton, 1998.

Animal Rites: Liturgies of Animal Care. London: SCM, 1999.

A world of Catholic reading at your fingertips ...

CTS

... now online
Browse 500 titles at

www.cts-online.org.uk

Catholic Faith, Life, and Truth for all